A Foundation Course in English

Practice Book 2

Ron Holt

Liz Hocking

New Edition

Macmillan Education
4 Crinan Street
London N1 9XW
A division of Springer Nature Ltd 1999
Companies and representatives throughout the world

www.macmillan.com

ISBN 978-1-4050-5853-7

Text © Ron Holt 1999 Liz Hocking 2004
Design and illustration © Springer Nature 1999

First published 1999
This edition published 2004

All rights reserved; no part of this publication may be
reproduced, stored in a retrieval system, transmitted in any
form or by any means, electronic, mechanical, photocopying,
recording or otherwise, without prior written permission
of the Publishers.

Illustrations by David Woodroffe

Printed and bound in The Netherlands by Wilco B.V.

2020
21

How to use this book

There are six workbooks in this series of practice books: *Way Ahead Practice Books 1* to *6*. They practise and support the grammar and vocabulary taught in *Way Ahead*.

This book can be used for homework or quiet time in the classroom, so it is largely self-access. In each exercise one example is usually given so that no presentation or explanation is required from the teacher. The rubrics are very similar in style to those in the course book and the grammar progression matches the course book exactly. No new material is presented and unknown vocabulary is completely avoided.

The material is arranged as 20 units to match the course books. Each unit practises the language taught in the corresponding unit in the Pupil's Book. The exercises should be done after the material in the Pupil's Book and the Workbook has been completed. The four-page Revision unit which begins the Practice Book reviews the structures and vocabulary taught in **Way Ahead 2**. Then there are two pages of exercises in each unit. There is a revision page after every unit. These can be used for consolidation, to check on class progress or as preparation for Workbook or school tests.

The types of exercise are similar to those in *Way Ahead Workbook 2*. They are carefully graded to match the level of the pupils and the emphasis is on writing words and sentences. There are no grammatical explanations but the target language is apparent in the exercises. The aim is to reinforce the learning of structures and vocabulary inductively.

At the end of the book there are 13 pages of handwriting practice which are graded to match the progression pupils are expected to make during the year. Revision of capital and small letter formation is followed by simple sentences practising capital letters, full stops, commas and question marks. Short poems, stories and factual prose are included to give more sustained writing practice.

Answers to exercises in this book are included in *Way Ahead Teacher's Book 2*.

Revision unit

a e i o u = **an**

1 Write.

1 What is this?   It's an insect.

2 What are these?   They're birds.

3 _____   _____

4 _____   _____

5 _____   _____

6 _____   _____

7 _____   _____

2 Write.

1 Is it an eye?   Yes, it is.

2 Are they hands?   Yes, they are.

3 _____   _____

4 _____   _____

5 _____   _____

6 _____   _____

7 _____   _____

3 Write.   am   is   are

1 I _am_ Sue. Meg _____ my friend. She _____ eight. I _____ seven. We _____ friends. We _____ happy.

2 Andy and Tom _____ friends. Andy _____ seven. Tom _____ six.

3 Fred _____ my baby brother. He _____ two.

4 Write.   have   has

We (1) _have_ a white house. It (2)_____ a big living room.

I (3)_____ a little bedroom. My mother and father (4)_____ a big bedroom.

I (5)_____ a doll. My brother (6)_____ a bike.

5 Write.   in   on   under   next to

1 The barn is _next to_ the house.   2 The tree is _____ the barn.

3 The horse is _____ the barn.   4 The goats are _____ the tree.

5 The hen is _____ the wall.   6 The birds are _____ the tree.

Revision unit

6 Look and write.

1 Is this his bag?   Yes, it is.

2 Are these her shorts?   No, they are not.

3 _____?      Yes, _____

4 _____?      No, _____

5 _____      No, _____

6 _____      Yes, _____

7 _____      Yes, _____

7 Read and draw.

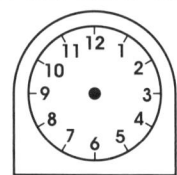      

1 It's half past seven.   2 It's four o'clock.   3 It's half past one.

8 Look and write.

1 _____   2 _____   3 _____

Revision unit

9 Read and tick (✓).

1 It can jump. ☐
   She can jump. ☐

2 He cannot fly. ☐
   It cannot fly. ☐

3 They are big. ☐
   It is big. ☐

10 Write.

1 <u>Can it</u> swim?  <u>Yes, it can.</u>

2 <u>Can they</u> fly?  <u>No, they cannot.</u>

3 _____ jump?  _____

4 _____ hop?  _____

5 _____ run?  _____

6 _____ walk?  _____

11 Read and draw lines.

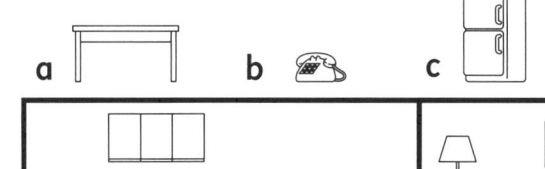

1 The phone is in the living room.
2 The table is in the kitchen.
3 The TV is in the living room.
4 The chair is in the bedroom.
5 The bed is in the bedroom.
6 The fridge is in the kitchen.

Revision unit

1 Good morning!

1 Write.   Hello   Good morning   I'm fine

Mr Wood: (1) Good morning , Tom. How are you?
Tom: (2) _____, Mr Wood. (3) _____, thank you.
Meg: (4) _____, Polly.
Polly: (5) _____, Meg.

2 Write.   flask   blackboard   ruler   desk   chair

1 What's this in English?   flask
2 What's this in English?   _____
3 What's this in English?   _____
4 What's this in English?   _____
5 What's this in English?   _____

3 Write.   Meg   Tom   Mr Macaroni   Pete   Polly

1 Who is this? It is Mr Macaroni .
2 Who is this? It is _____.
3 Who is this? It is _____.
4 Who is this? It is _____.
5 Who is this? It is _____.

Identifying

4 Write.   What   Who

1  <u>Who</u> is this?
It's Andy.

2  <u>What</u> is this?
It's a train.

3  _____ is this?
It's a van.

4  _____ is this?
It's Grandfather.

5  _____ is this?
It's Grandmother.

6 _____ is this?
It's a plane.

5 Draw.

Draw a bird on the table.
Draw a chair next to the table.
Draw a cat under the chair.
Draw a box under the table.
Draw a cat in the box.

6 Read and find.

l	d	p	**m**	o	n	k	e	y	u
u	m	**b**	o	x	l	l	**h**	a	t
y	**u**	m	b	r	e	l	l	a	z
c	k	**c**	h	a	i	r	q	e	r

Write

1 <u>monkey</u>

2 _____   3 _____

4 _____

5 _____

Revision Unit 1

1 Write.

1 What is this?      It is a chair.

2 Who is this?   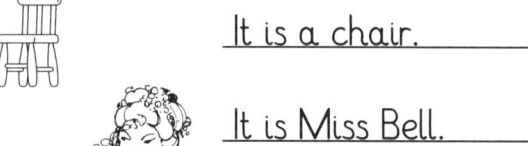   It is Miss Bell.

3 _____ is this?

4 _____ is this?

5 _____ is this?

6 _____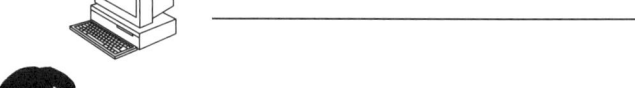

7 _____

2 Read and colour.

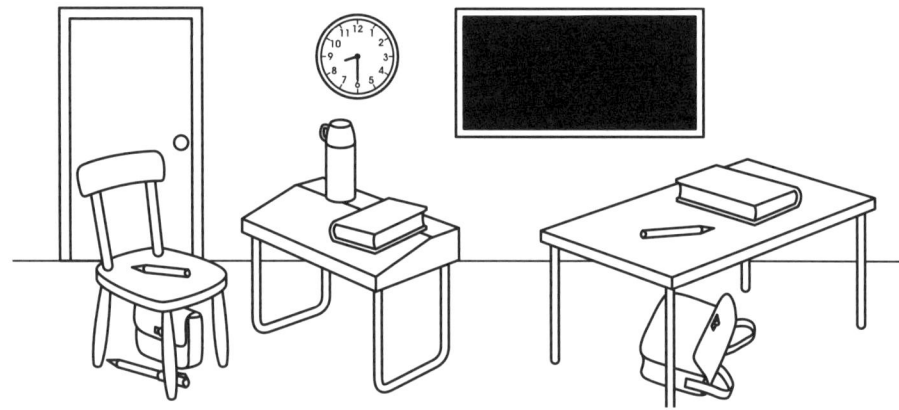

There is a green flask on the desk. There is a red pencil on the chair. There is a blue bag under the chair. There is a yellow book on the table.

3 Write.

The pen is (1)_____ the chair. The clock is (2)_____ the blackboard and the door. What is the time? It is (3)_____.

Revision Unit 1

This is my family.

1 Read and write.

Andy is eight. He has a brother.
He's one. He has a sister. She's one.
His brother and sister are twins.

1 How old is Andy? _____
2 How old is his brother? _____
3 How old is his sister? _____

2 Write.   am   is   are

My name (1)_____ Tom. I (2)_____ seven. Andy (3)_____ my friend.
He (4)_____ eight. We (5)_____ friends. Andy's brother and sister
(6)_____ twins. They're one. How old (7)_____ you? (8)_____ you one?

3 Write.   That   Those

1 This is a balloon. _That_ is a ball.

2 This is a flag. _____ is a kite.

3 These are dolls. _____ are robots.

4 _____ are computer games. These are CDs.

Identifying **11**

4 Read and find.

e	t	**r**	o	b	o	t	o	r	m	e	r	o
n	**c**	a	r	h	k	**p**	l	a	n	e	g	v
d	**t**	a	x	i	u	**t**	o	y	s	y	d	t
h	**g**	r	a	n	d	m	o	t	h	e	r	d

Write.

1 robot
2 _____   3 _____
4 _____   5 _____
6 _____

5 Read and colour.

1  This cat is brown. That cat is black.

2  That kite is red. This kite is blue.

3  Those balloons are yellow. These balloons are green.

6 Write

mother   father   sister   brother
grandmother   grandfather

1 grandmother

2 _____

3 _____

4 _____

5 _____   6 _____

12 Family

Revision Unit 2

1 Write. this   that   these   those

1. _____ is my teddy and _____ are my dolls. _____ are my books and _____ is my desk.

2. _____ is my father and _____ are my sisters. _____ is my mother and _____ are my brothers.

3. _____ are his socks and _____ is his hat.

4. _____ are his trousers and _____ is his bike.

5. _____ is his T-shirt and _____ are his shoes.

2 Write about Tico.

(1)_____ is it? It (2)_____ Tico!
Tico (3)_____ a clown.
His shoes (4)_____ big.
His bike (5)_____ small.
His trousers (6)_____ red and yellow.

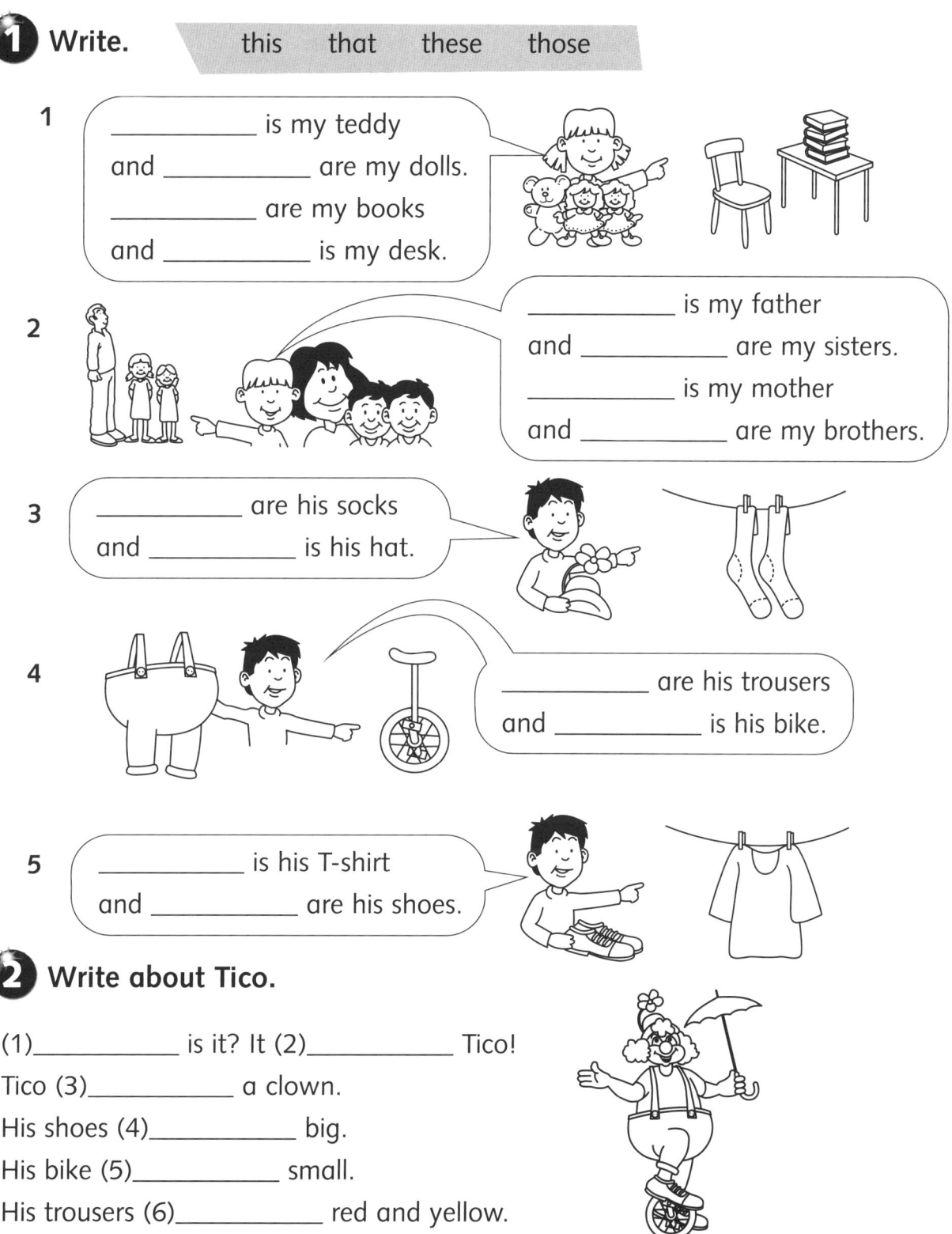

3 We like sweets.

1 Read and find.

q	r	**c**	a	k	e	s	y	u	s	e
d	**s**	w	e	e	t	s	k	y	q	f
e	**l**	o	l	l	i	p	o	p	s	t
d	w	**b**	i	s	c	u	i	t	s	e

Write.

1 <u>cakes</u>
2 _____
3 _____
4 _____

2 Write.

like   don't like

1 ✓ 🧁 I _____ cakes.   2 ✗ 🍭 I _____ lollipops.
3 ✗ 🍬 I _____ sweets.   4 ✓ 🍪 I _____ biscuits.
5 ✓ 🍬🧁 I like _____ and I like _____, too.
6 ✓ 🍬🍭 I _____ and I _____
7 ✓ 🍬🍪 _____
8 ✓ 🧁🍭 _____

3 Look and write the words.

1  sneka   2 odg

3  spedir   4 nloi

5  atc   6  phelante

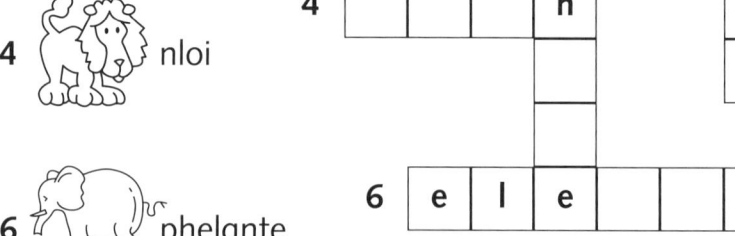

Like/do not like

4 Write.

1 Do you like cats? ✓ — Yes, I do.
2 Do you like dogs? ✗ — No, I don't.
3 Do you like spiders? ✗ — _____
4 Do you like snakes? ✓ — _____
5 Do you like lions? ✓ — _____
6 Do you like elephants? ✗ — _____

5 Look and write.

1 elephants ✗ spiders ✗
2 dogs ✗ cats ✗
3 lions ✗ snakes ✗

We don't like elephants or _____.
We _____ or _____.
_____

4 elephants ✓ spiders ✗
5 cats ✓ dogs ✓
6 lions ✓ snakes ✗

We like elephants but we don't like _____.
We _____ and _____.
_____

6 Read and tick (✓) or cross (✗).

We don't like snakes but we like spiders.
We don't like snakes or dogs.
We like lions but we don't like snakes.

snakes ☐ spiders ☐
snakes ☐ dogs ☐
lions ☐ snakes ☐

4 I like football.

1 Write.

	1	s	w					
		p						
2	f	o						
3	r	i						
		t						
4	b	a	s					

2 Write.   Yes, I do.   No, I don't.

1 Do you like drawing? _____
2 Do you like football? _____
3 Do you like basketball? _____
4 Do you like swimming? _____
5 Do you like riding? _____
6 Do you like reading? _____

3 Write.

1 Meg   reading      Meg likes reading.
2 Sue   singing   _____
3 Tom   watching TV   _____
4 Billy   drawing   _____
5 Pete   reading   _____

Activities 17

4 Look and write.

Sue — ball ✓ / football ✗
Tom — TV ✓ / swimming ✓
Andy — singing ✗ / drawing ✗
Pete — book ✓ / riding ✓
Polly — football ✗ / swimming ✗
Meg — riding ✓ / ball ✗

1 Does Meg like riding?   Yes, she _does_.
2 Does Polly like swimming?   No, she _doesn't_.
3 Does Tom like watching TV?   Yes, he _____.
4 Does Andy like singing?   No, he _____.
5 Do Meg and Pete like riding?   _____
6 Do Sue and Polly like football? _____

5 Look and write.

1 Tom likes _____ and _____.
2 Pete _____.
3 Andy _____ or _____.
4 Polly _____.
5 Sue likes _____ but _____.
6 Meg _____.

6 Look and write.   her   his   my

1 This is _____ T-shirt.
2 These are _____ shorts.
3 This is _____ hat.
4 This is _____ skirt.
5 This is _____ basketball.
6 This is _____ football.

18 Activities

Revision Unit 4

1 Look and write.

Sam ✓ basketball ✗ singing ✗ swimming ✗ drawing

Jane ✗ basketball ✗ singing ✓ reading ✓ swimming

1 Does Sam like basketball?
_____

Does Sam like drawing?
_____

Does Sam like singing?
_____

2 Does Jane like basketball?
_____

Does Jane like singing?
_____

Does Jane like reading?
_____

2 Write.

1 _____ computer games? — Yes, I _____.
2 _____ Jane like basketball? — No, _____.
3 _____ Sam like singing? — No, _____.
4 _____ like swimming? — No, I _____.
5 _____ like computer games? — Yes, we _____.
6 _____ singing? — No, we _____.

3 Read and tick (✓) or cross (✗).

1 Sam likes playing computer games and basketball. ☐ 💻 ☐ 🏀
2 He doesn't like singing or drawing. ☐ 🎵 ☐ ✏️

Look and write.

3 Jane _____. ✓ 📖 ✓ 🏊
4 She _____. ✗ 🏀 ✗ 🎵

Revision Unit 4 19

5 This is our school.

1 Read and colour.

1. Our hair is brown.
   Their hair is yellow.

2. Their hats are red.
   Our hats are green.

3. Our car is blue.
   Their car is purple.

2 Write.

our   their

1. They have a big house.
   Their house is big.
   We have a small house.
   Our house is small.

2. We have a black cat.
   _____ cat is black.
   They have a white cat.
   _____ cat is white.

3. They have a big school.
   _____ school is big.
   We have a small school.
   _____ school is small.

4. We have a white car.
   _____ car is white.
   They have a black car.
   _____ car is black.

Describing

3 Write.

Bill	riding	
Lisa	swimming	
Mick	reading	
Pat	drawing	
Fred	singing	

1 His name is Mick. <u>He likes reading.</u>

2 His name is Fred. _____

3 Her name is Lisa. _____

4 His name is Bill. _____

5 Her name is Pat. _____

4 Write.

	cats	dogs	birds	fish	frogs	snakes	spiders
Meg	✓		✓		✗	✗	
Tom		✓			✓	✗	✗
Sue			✓	✓	✗		✗
Andy		✓				✗	
Lisa	✓						✗
Billy	✓	✗					

1 Meg <u>likes cats and birds. She doesn't like frogs or snakes.</u>

2 Tom _____

3 Sue _____

4 Andy <u>likes dogs but he doesn't like</u> _____

5 Lisa _____

6 Billy _____

Revision

Revision Unit 5

1 Look, read and write.   our   their

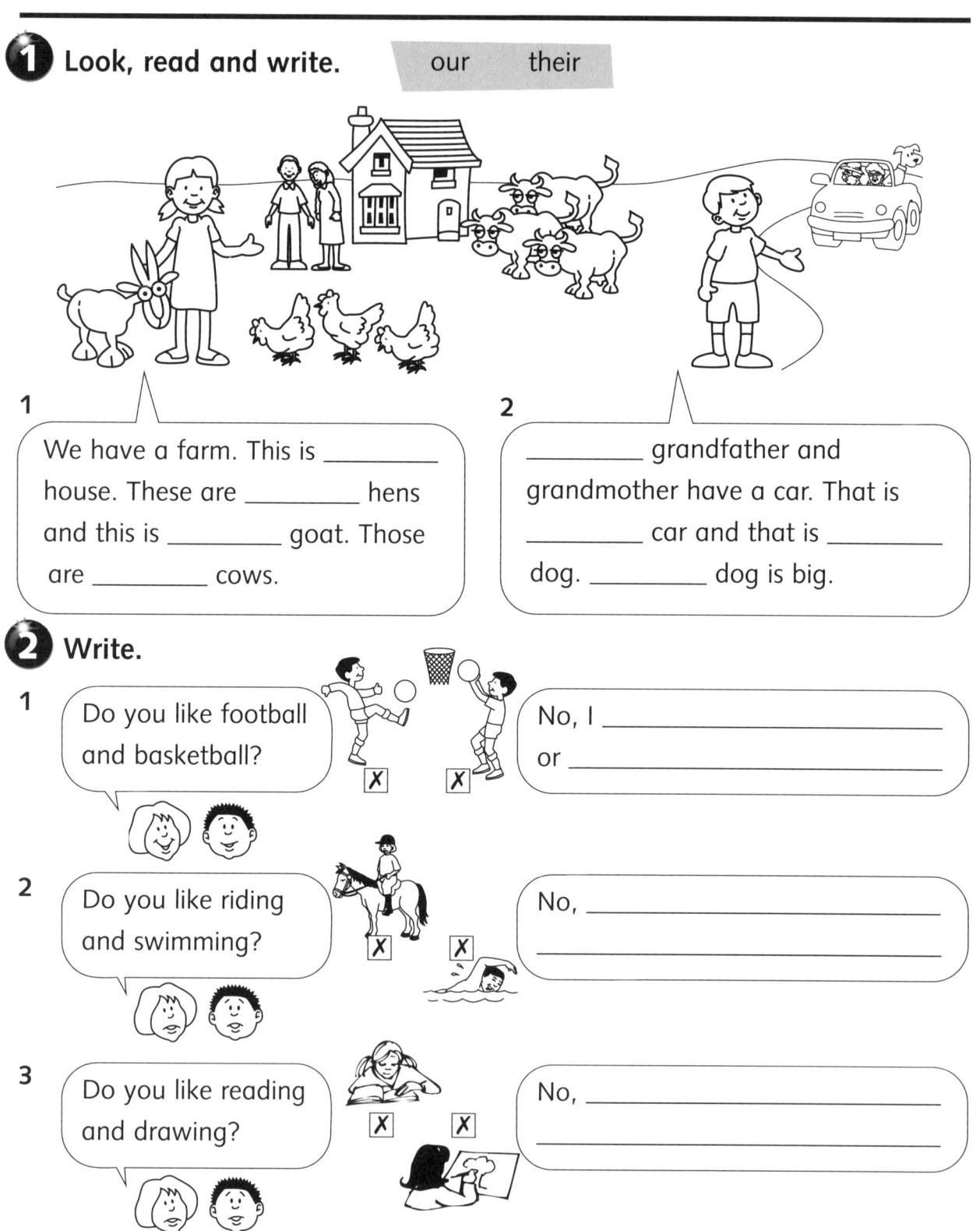

1. We have a farm. This is _____ house. These are _____ hens and this is _____ goat. Those are _____ cows.

2. _____ grandfather and grandmother have a car. That is _____ car and that is _____ dog. _____ dog is big.

2 Write.

1. Do you like football and basketball?   No, I _____ or _____

2. Do you like riding and swimming?   No, _____

3. Do you like reading and drawing?   No, _____

6 He has an umbrella!

1 Read and find.   Write

q	c	i	r	c	u	s	f	b	i	k	e
s	g	l	a	s	s	e	s	t	y	e	d
w	u	m	b	r	e	l	l	a	f	r	z
a	c	x	v	b	a	b	i	e	s	k	l

1 _circus_   2 _____
3 _____
4 _____
5 _____

2 Write.   have   has

Ricky (1) _has_____ a brother, Dan. He doesn't (2)_____ a sister.
Ricky and Dan are on the beach. They (3)_____ a ball.
Ricky is in the water. He (4)_____ the ball.
Their mother and father are on the beach, too.
They (5)_____ an umbrella.

3 Write.

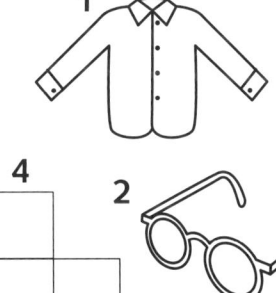

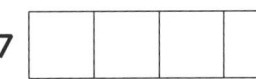

Clothing 23

4 Read and write.   do   don't   does   doesn't

> Uncle Bob has a red beard. He has a hat. Aunt Jane has blond hair. She has a green bag.

1 <u>Does</u> Uncle Bob have a beard? Yes, he _____.

2 _____ Aunt Jane have a beard? No, she _____.

3 _____ Uncle Bob and Aunt Jane have black hair?
   No, they _____.

4 _____ Uncle Bob have a hat? Yes, he _____.

5 _____ Aunt Jane have a blue bag? No, she _____.

5 Draw and colour.

I have black curly hair.
I have brown eyes.
I have a small nose.

She has straight brown hair.
She has blue eyes.
She has a big nose.

6 Write about you.

My hair	My eyes	My nose
long short straight curly black brown blonde	brown grey blue	big small

My hair is _____.

My eyes are _____. My nose is _____.

Describing people

Revision Unit 6

1 Look and write.

A

B

C

D

E

F

| has | have | doesn't have | don't have |

1 I'm Milly. I _____ long, straight hair. I _____ glasses. ☐
2 My brothers _____ glasses, too. They _____ curly, blonde hair. ☐
3 Aunt Peggy _____ curly, black hair. She _____ glasses. ☐
4 My cousins _____ black, curly hair. They _____ straight, blonde hair. ☐
5 My friend Anna _____ straight, black hair. She _____ glasses. ☐
6 Anna's sisters _____ glasses. They _____ straight hair. It is blonde and curly. ☐

2 Complete the questions. Write the answers.

1 _____ Anna have glasses?   _____

2 _____ Milly have black hair?   _____

3 _____ Milly's cousins have glasses?  _____

4 _____ you have curly hair? _____

Revision Unit 6

I get up at 7 o'clock.

1 Match and write the number.

have breakfast ☐

brush hair ☐

get up ☐

say goodbye ☐

wash face ☐

go to school ☐

brush teeth ☐

2 Write.

 1   I <u>wash my face</u> at <u>7 o'clock</u>.

 2   I _____ then _____.

 3   I _____.

 4   I _____ then _____.

 5   I _____.

3 Write.

1 _____   2 _____   3 _____

Sequencing events

4 Read and write.

wake   have   go   play   watch   do   wakes
has   goes   plays   watches   does

My name is Tom.
I wake up at six o'clock.
I have breakfast.
Then I go to school.
In the afternoon I play with my friends.
Then I watch TV.
In the evening I do my homework.
I go to bed at nine o'clock.

His name is Tom

1 He _wakes_ up.
2 He _____ breakfast.
3 He _____ to school.
4 He _____ with his friends.
5 He _____ TV.
6 He _____ his homework.
7 He _____ to bed.

5 Read and write.

close   count   yawn   stretch   jump   touch   closes
counts   yawns   stretches   jumps   touches

I close my eyes.
I count to ten.
I yawn and stretch.
I yawn again.
I jump out of bed.
And touch my toes.

1 She _closes_ her eyes.
2 She _____ to ten.
3 She _____ and _____.
4 She _____ again.
5 She _____ out of bed.
6 She _____ her toes.

6 Draw and write.

1
I go to school at
_____.

2
I go home at
_____.

3
I watch TV at
_____.

4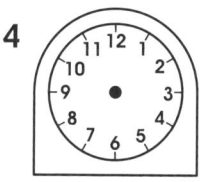
I go to bed at
_____.

Sequencing events

Revision Unit 7

1 Look, read and write.

Andy	Meg	Tom	Sue	Polly	Pete
____	____	morning	____	____	____

1 (In the morning I have breakfast and then I brush my teeth.)   Tom
2 (I play basketball in the afternoon and then I do my homework.)   _____
3 (In the evening I watch TV and then I do my homework.)   _____
4 (I do my homework in the evening and then I go to bed.)   _____
5 (In the morning I have breakfast and then I brush my hair.)   _____
6 (In the afternoon I do my homework and then I watch TV.)   _____

2 Answer and write the questions.

1 When does Sue do her homework? _____

2 When does Pete do his homework? _____

3 When _____? She does her homework in the evening.

4 When _____? He does his homework in the afternoon.

5 When do you do your homework? _____

8 What is her job?

1 Read and find.   Write.

d	**n**	u	r	s	e	w	d	o	f	n	u
z	**s**	h	o	p	k	e	e	p	e	r	r
v	y	l	**w**	a	i	t	e	r	g	b	a
d	k	s	u	**t**	e	a	c	h	e	r	t	z
f	d	l	k	**d**	o	c	t	o	r	h	j

1 _nurse_
2 _____
3 _____
4 _____
5 _____

2 Write   school   hospital   shop   cafe

1 She's a doctor. <u>She works in a hospital</u>.

2 She's a nurse. _____.

3 He's a shopkeeper. _____.

4 He's a waiter. _____.

5 She's a teacher. _____.

3 Write.   by car   by bike   by taxi   on foot   by bus

1 He doesn't go to work by bus. He goes to work <u>by car</u>.

2 She doesn't go to school _____. She goes to school _____.

3 She doesn't go to town _____. _____.

4 He doesn't go to school _____. _____.

5 She doesn't go to work _____. _____.

Travelling 29

4 Write.

riding   walking   driving

1 She walks to school.   She likes <u>walking</u>.

2 He drives his car to work.   He likes _____ his car.

3 He rides his bike to school.   He likes _____ his bike.

5 Write.

swimming   play   watches   help   fishing
their   his   my   his   my

1 I like helping _____ mother. I <u>help</u> her on Saturday and Sunday.

2 They _____ basketball on Monday. This is _____ basketball.

3 He _____ TV on Saturday. This is _____ TV.

4 I can swim. I go _____ on Tuesday. This is _____ swimsuit.

5 My father fishes in his boat. He goes _____ on Wednesday. This is _____ boat.

6 Write the question. Complete the answer.

like   don't like

1 Does she like _____?   ✓   Yes, she does.

2 Does he like _____?   ✗   No, he doesn't.

3 Do _____?   ✓   Yes, I do.

4 _____?   ✓   Yes, we _____.

5 _____?   ✗   No, _____.

6 _____?   ✗   _____

Days of the week/travelling

Revision Unit 8

1 Look and read.

Anna is a nurse. She works in the hospital. She does not like cars or buses. She likes walking. She goes to work on foot. She goes to work at half past seven. On Tuesday she plays basketball. On Sunday she helps her grandmother.

2 Answer the questions.

1 What is Anna's job? _____

2 Where does she work? _____

3 Does she like cars? _____

4 How does she go to work? _____

5 When does she go to work? _____

6 When does she play basketball? _____

7 When does she help her grandmother? _____

3 Write what is wrong.

1
Anna is not a doctor.

2
_____

3
_____

4
_____

9 I'm in front of Tom.

1 Write. in   on   under   behind   between   in front of

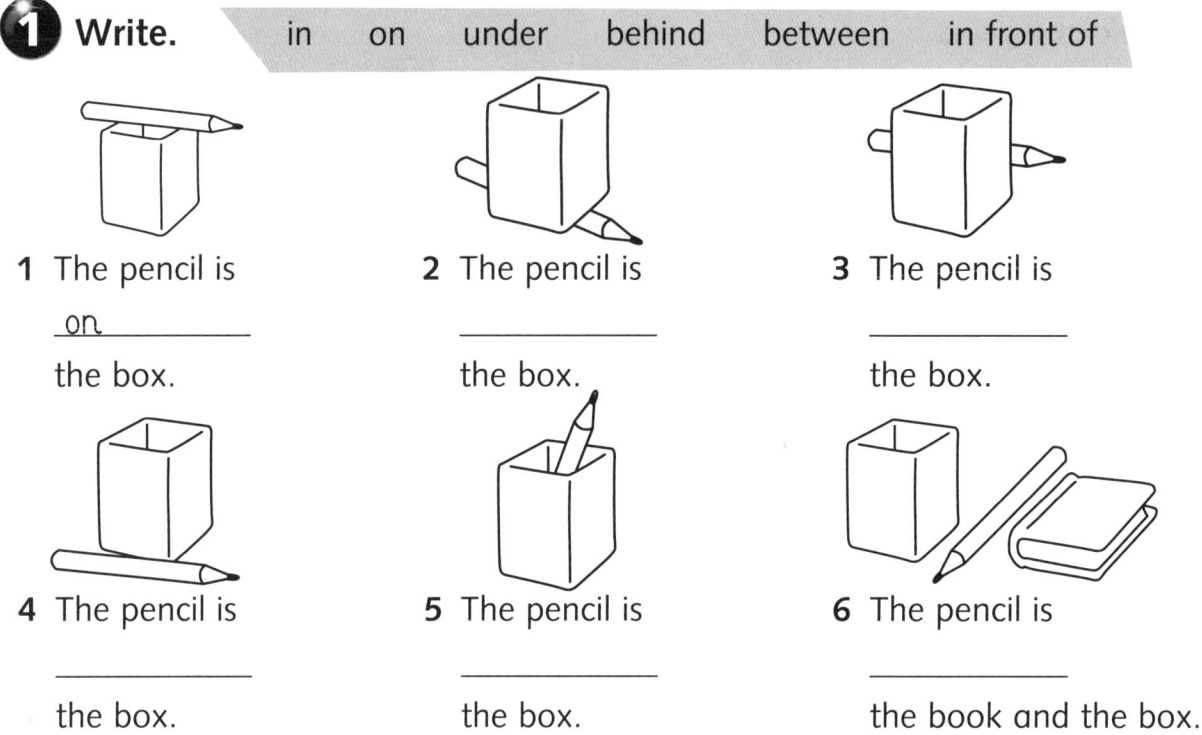

1 The pencil is _on_ the box.

2 The pencil is _____ the box.

3 The pencil is _____ the box.

4 The pencil is _____ the box.

5 The pencil is _____ the box.

6 The pencil is _____ the book and the box.

2 Read, colour and write.

The big green pencil is on the left. The small blue pencil is on the right.
The big yellow pencil is on the right. The purple pencil is next to the blue pencil.
The small orange pencil is on the left. The red pencil is next to the green pencil.

1 Where is the yellow pencil? _It is on the right_____.

2 Where is the red pencil? _____.

3 Where is the orange pencil? _____.

4 Where is the purple pencil? _____.

Describing position

3 Read and find.

s	g	**c**	a	s	t	l	e	f	**h**	i	l	l
v	z	**l**	e	m	o	n	a	d	e	w	u	b
m	u	p	**p**	r	i	n	c	e	s	s	r	j
d	**b**	r	i	d	g	e	a	**t**	r	e	e	c

Write

1 <u>castle</u> 2 _____
3 _____
4 _____
5 _____ 6 _____

4 Write.   eat   touch   drink   run   walk

1 She runs in school.   Do not <u>run</u> in school.
2 He touches dogs.   Do not _____ dogs.
3 He drinks lemonade.   Do not _____ lemonade.
4 She eats sweets.   Do not _____ sweets.
5 He walks on the flowers.   Do not _____ on the flowers.

5 Write.   slowly   quickly   quietly   loudly

1 The horse is old. It is very slow. It is walking <u>slowly</u>.
2 I cannot hear you. Please speak _____.
3 The mouse is small. The cat is here. The mouse runs very _____.
4 The baby is sleeping. Speak _____.

Adverbs

Revision Unit 9

1 Look, read and write.

1 Who is next to the horse? _____
2 What is on the hill? _____
3 What is behind the tree? _____
4 Who is in front of the castle? _____
5 What is in front of the tree? _____

2 Read and tick (✓) or cross (✗).

1 The tree is on the right. ☐
2 Princess is behind the castle. ☐
3 The cat is in the tree. ☐
4 The cat is on the right. ☐
5 The castle is on the left. ☐
6 The dog is next to the horse. ☐

3 Look and write.

play football   swim   run   talk   touch

1 Do not _____ here!
2 _____ here!
3 _____ in school!
4 _____ in class!
5 _____!

10 I can see you!

1 Write. Yes, I can. No, I can't. Yes, I am. No, I'm not.

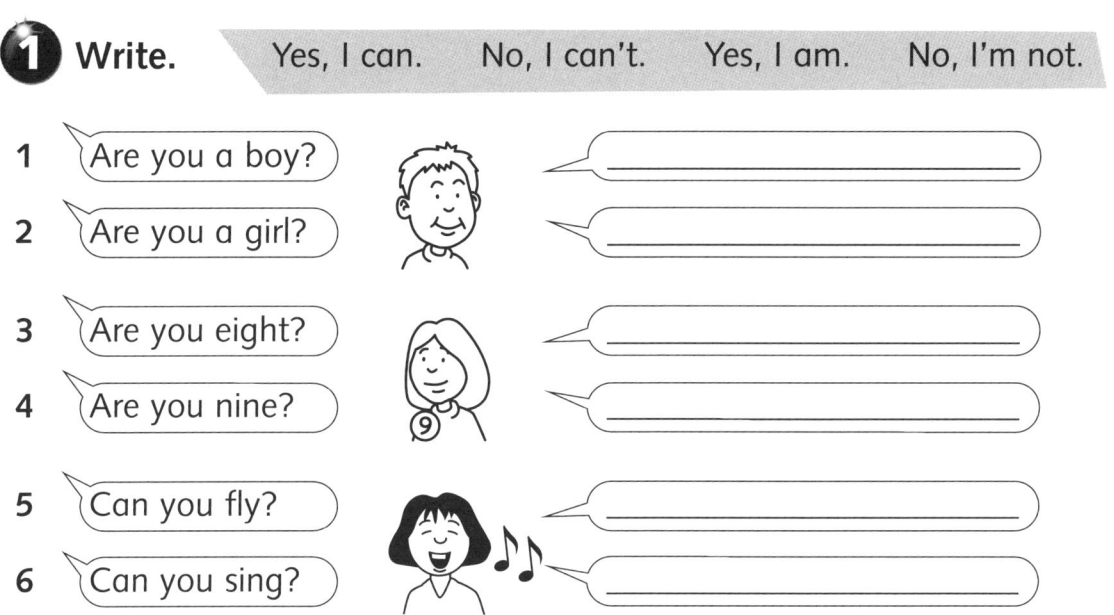

1 Are you a boy? _____
2 Are you a girl? _____
3 Are you eight? _____
4 Are you nine? _____
5 Can you fly? _____
6 Can you sing? _____

2 Read and write.

1 Can a snake run? No, it can't.   2 Can a bird fly? _____
3 Can a frog jump? _____   4 Can a spider swim? _____
5 Can a cat fly? _____   6 Can a fish swim? _____

3 Write.   him   her   it

1 Can you see the blackboard? I can see it .
2 Can you see the teacher?   I can see _____ .
3 Can you see Meg?   I can see _____ .
4 Can you see Tom?   I can see _____ .
5 Can you see the book?   I can see _____ .

Abilities

4 Write.

> is   goes   has   goes   goes
> comes   watches   works   gets

1 Mr Brown _is_____ a waiter. He _____ up at eight o'clock.
   He _____ to work at eight o'clock.
2 He _____ to work by bus. He _____ all day.
   He _____ home at eight o'clock. He _____ his dinner.
   He _____ TV. He _____ to bed at eleven o'clock.

5 Write.

> me   you   him

1 Look at _____! Listen to _____!

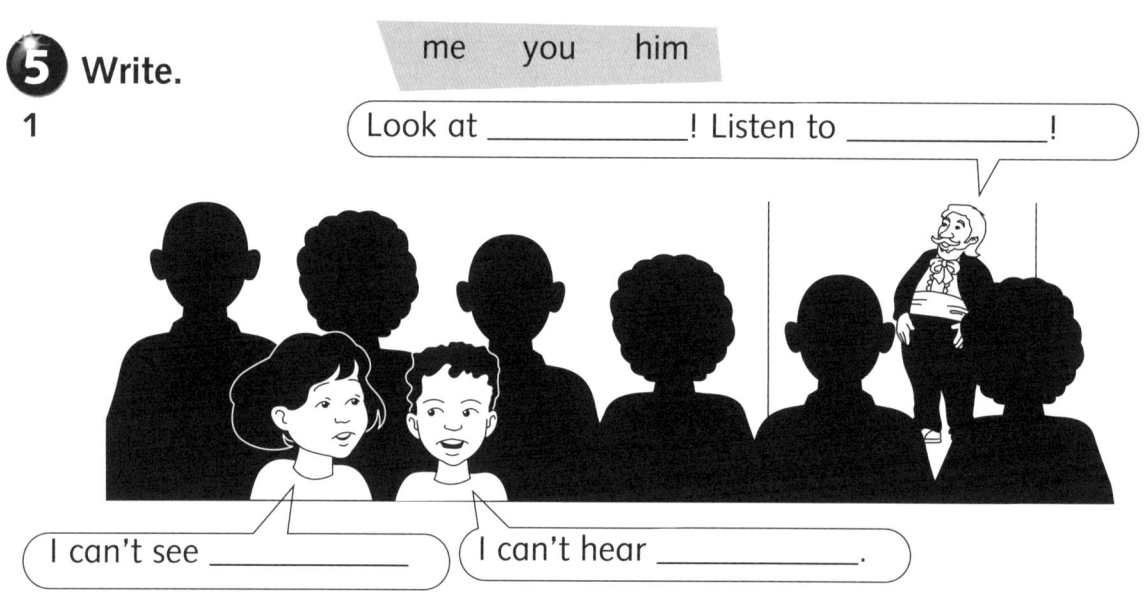

I can't see _____   I can't hear _____.

2 Can I read to _____?   Yes. Sit next to _____

3 Can we play with _____?

Revision

Revision Unit 10

1 Read and write.　　him　her　it

1 Tom likes Andy. He plays football with _____. Tom doesn't play basketball. He doesn't like _____.

2 Sue doesn't like football. She plays basketball. She likes _____. Sue runs quickly. Polly likes playing with _____.

3 Pete has a horse. He can ride _____. Meg can ride. Pete goes riding with _____.

2 Write the answers.

1 Does Sue like football?　　　　No, Sue does not like football.
2 Does Tom like basketball?　　　_____
3 Who does Polly like playing with?　_____
4 Who does Tom like?　　　　　_____
5 What can Pete ride?　　　　　_____
6 Who does Pete go riding with?　_____

3 Write the answers.

1 Do you like football?　　　　Yes, I do.
2 Does Tom like basketball?　　_____
3 Does Sue run slowly?　　　　_____
4 Do you like football?　　　　_____

11 Where do they come from?

1 Write.   English   Arabic   Chinese

1 Fuad comes from Egypt. He speaks _____.
_____ in a big city.

2 Ann comes from America. She speaks _____.
_____ on a farm.

3 Li comes from China. She speaks _____.
_____ in a town.

4 Sam comes from Australia. He speaks _____.
_____ in a city.

2 Write about you.

My name is _____. I come from _____.
I speak _____. I live in _____.

3 Read and find.   Write.

v	r	**p**	a	n	d	a	r	w	o	l
b	e	t	**w**	h	a	l	e	p	y	m
c	k	i	**p**	a	r	r	o	t	h	r
v	**c**	r	o	c	o	d	i	l	e	t
h	e	**p**	e	n	g	u	i	n	n	l
j	y	o	p	h	**s**	n	a	k	e	f

1 <u>panda</u>
2 _____
3 _____
4 _____
5 _____
6 _____

38 Countries and animals

4 Match and write the number.

forest ☐   snow ☐   sea ☐   river ☐   mountains ☐   desert ☐

5 What lives here? Write the words.

forest	snow	sea	river	mountains	desert
				pandas	

6 Write.

1 <u>Pandas live in the mountains.</u>

2 _____

3 _____

4 _____

5 _____

6 _____

7 Write.   big   hot   beautiful   sharp   cold

Whales are very (1) <u>big</u>. Snow is very (2)_____.
Parrots are (3)_____. Crocodiles have very (4)_____
teeth. Snakes like (5)_____ deserts.

Animals and locations

Revision Unit 11

1 Write.

1. river
2. desert
3. sea
4. snow
5. mountains
6. forest
7. city
8. farm

2 Where are they from? Write.

America   Australia   China   Egypt   England

1. Ahmed _____
2. Linda _____
3. Scott _____
4. Todd _____
5. Li _____

3 Read and tick (✓) or cross (✗).

1 Ahmed speaks Chinese. ✗
2 Camels live in the sea. ☐
3 Linda lives in a small town. ☐
4 Li comes from China. ☐
5 Pandas live in the mountains. ☐
6 Scott comes from America. ☐

Write what is wrong. Write the correct sentence.

1 <u>Ahmed does not speak Chinese. He speaks Arabic.</u>
2 _____
3 _____

12 Do you have any bananas?

1 Look and write the words.

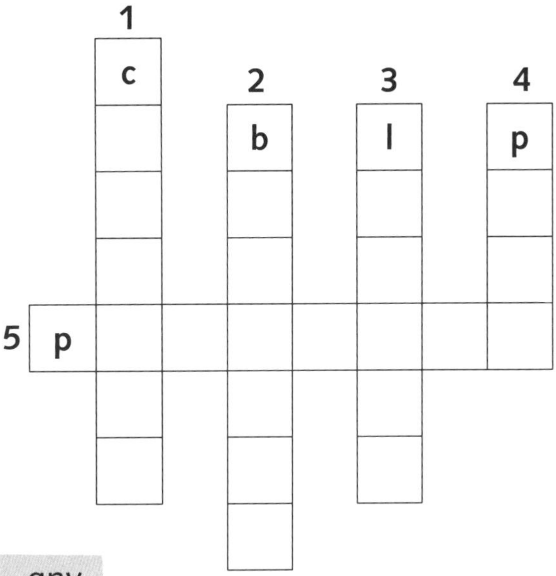

1. (carrots)
2. (bananas)
3. (lemons)
4. (peas)
5. (potatoes)

Crossword: 1 c, 2 b, 3 l, 4 p, 5 p

2 Write. some any

Do you have (1) _any_ bananas?

Yes, I have (2) _____ bananas.

Do you have (3) _____ strawberries?

I'm sorry. I have (4) _____ nice bananas.
I don't have (5) _____ strawberries.

Do you have (6) _____ melons?

I'm sorry. I don't have (7) _____.

3 Read and find.   Write.

a	**a**	p	p	l	e	v	**p**	e	a	r	c
w	**s**	t	r	a	w	b	e	r	r	y	o
s	r	**m**	e	l	o	n	f	s	z	w	y
a	**o**	r	a	n	g	e	**g**	r	a	p	e

1 _apple_   2 _____
3 _____
4 _____
5 _____   6 _____

Shopping/enquiring

4 Write.

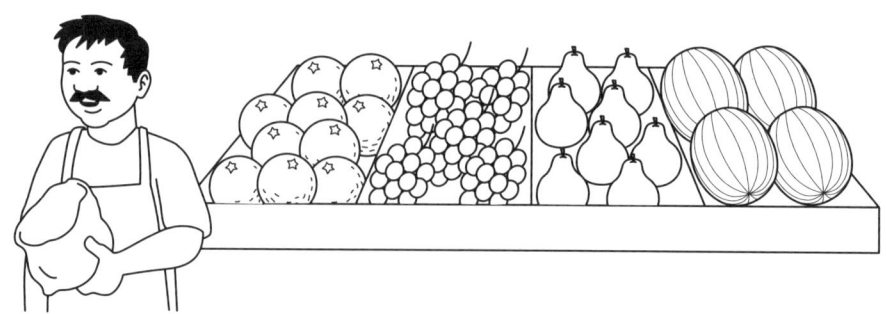

1 Does he have any oranges? <u>Yes, he has some oranges.</u>
2 Does he have any potatoes? <u>No, he doesn't have any potatoes.</u>
3 Does he have any melons? _____
4 Does he have any grapes? _____
5 Does he have any carrots? _____
6 Does he have any peas? _____

5 Read and write.   want   have   some   any

1 Do you <u>want any</u> peas?
2 Yes. I <u>want some</u> peas, please. Do you _____ bananas?
3 No, I don't, but I _____ grapes.
4 I don't _____ grapes, thank you.
5 Do you _____ oranges?
6 Yes. I _____ oranges, please. Do you _____ lemons?
7 Yes, I do. I _____ nice lemons.

Want/don't want

Revision Unit 12

1 Write. Read and match.   some   any

1. I don't have _____ strawberries.
I have _____ melons and
I have _____ carrots. I don't
have _____ bananas. I have
_____ potatoes.

2. I have _____ apples and
I have _____ pears. I don't
have _____ grapes but
I have _____ carrots.
Do you have _____ grapes?

Mr Black ☐   Mrs White ☐   Mr Brown ☐

2 Write.   does   doesn't   do   don't

1 Does Mr Black have any carrots?   Yes, he _____.
2 Does Mr Brown have any melons?   _____
3 Does Mrs White have any bananas? _____

4 (Do you have any oranges?)   _____
5 (Do you have any grapes?)   _____
6 (Do you have any carrots?)   _____

3 What does Mr Green want? Look and write.

apples
oranges ✗
potatoes ✗
grapes
strawberries
carrots ✗

I want _____.
I don't want _____.
_____
_____
_____

13 What is the weather like?

1 Write.   cloudy   wet   windy   sunny   hot   cold   snowy   foggy

1 It is _cold_.   2 It is _____.   3 It is _____.

4 It is _____.   5 It is _____.

6 It is _____.   7 It is _____.   8 It is _____.

2 Write.

1 It is _____ and _____.   2 _____

3 _____   4 _____

3 Write the letters.

M   J   F   A   S   O   D   N

January   __ebruary   __arch   __pril   __ay   __une

__uly   __ugust   __eptember   __ctober   __ovember   __ecember

44 Describing weather

4 Write.

1. (22) twenty-two
2. (___) sixty
3. (___) thirty-seven
4. (46) _____
5. (55) _____
6. (___) sixty-three
7. (___) seventy-eight
8. (81) _____
9. (94) _____
10. (100) _____
11. (___) thirty-two
12. (___) forty

5 Write the words and the numbers.

Sam   Billy   Ann   Ben   Jane   Dan

1. Ben is number _thirty-one_.
2. Ann is number ninety-nine.
3. Dan is number fifty.
4. Sam is number _____.
5. Jane is number _____.
6. Billy is number sixty-seven.

6 Write.

big   small   nice   hot   cold

1. Our country is _____.
2. Our school is _____.
3. Our teacher is _____.
4. Ice cream is _____.

Numbers 45

Revision Unit 13

1 Write.

1 T- sh_rt   2 _ack_t   3 s_ng_asse_   4 b_ _ts

5 sh_ _ts   6 h_t   7 u_bre_la   8 s_cks   9 s_oes

2 Look at the words above. Write in the correct bags.

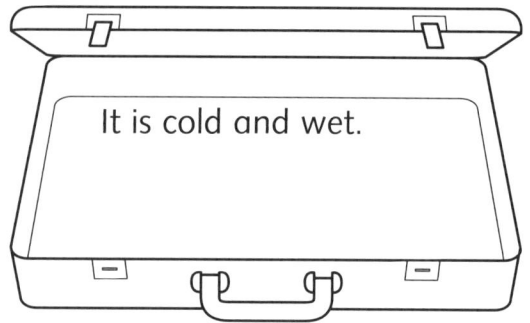

It is cold and wet.

It is hot and sunny.
T-shirt

3 What is the weather like? Write and match.

1 Wear your jacket. It's _____.   A

2 Wear your sunglasses. It's _____.   B

3 Wear your T-shirt. It's _____.   C

4 Wear your hat. It's _____.   D

5 Take your umbrella. It's _____.   E

14 There are lots of people.

1 Read and find.

d	**m**	a	n	x	**b**	o	y	k	o
s	w	**p**	e	o	p	l	e	w	e
z	b	v	d	**w**	o	m	a	n	g
n	**b**	a	b	y	e	**g**	i	r	l
z	**c**	h	i	l	d	r	e	n	h

Write.

1 _man_ 2 _____
3 _____
4 _____
5 _____ 6 _____
7 _____

2 Write.

1 one child two _children_
2 one baby two _____
3 one girl two _____
4 one boy two _____
5 one man two _____
6 one woman two _____

3 Write.

is   are

1 In the playground there _is_ a slide. There _____ some swings. On the swings there _____ three girls. Next to the swings there _____ a woman.

2 In the park there _____ a man and a dog. There _____ two boys on bikes.

3 There _____ some trees. Two babies _____ under the trees. Next to the pond there _____ some boys. There _____ a boat in the pond.

Describing a scene

4 Draw and colour.

There is a yellow pencil on the table. There are two books. One is green and one is blue. There is a long ruler between the books and the pencil. There is a red bag under the table and there are two orange books on the bag.

5 Look and write.

1 Are there any hats? Yes, there are.
  How many hats are there? There are three.

2 Are there any socks? No, there are not.

3 Are there any jackets? _____
  How many _____? _____

4 Are there any shoes? _____?
  _____? There are _____.

5 Are there any T-shirts? _____

Write the questions.

6 _____? There are two.

7 _____? There is one.

Describing a scene

Revision Unit 14

1 Look, read and write the number.

1. There is a boat on the pond. There are two children next to the pond. There are three men on bikes. There are two women next to the swings.

2. There is a boat on the pond. There are two babies on the swings. There are two children next to the pond. There are two men on bikes.

3. There are two boats on the pond. There are three children on bikes. There are three women under the tree. There are two men next to the slide.

4. There are two children on bikes. There are three men under the tree. There are two boats on the pond. There is a slide in the playground.

2 Read, write and colour.   a   the

There are two cats on the wall.

There is (1)_____ big cat and there is (2)_____ small cat. (3)_____ big cat is grey and (4)_____ small cat is orange.

15 Whose ring is this?

1 Read and find.

s	b	**g**	l	a	s	s	e	s	d	d	o
a	**t**	r	a	i	n	e	r	s	f	g	p
z	**w**	a	t	c	h	e	**r**	i	n	g	v
z	**c**	o	m	b	t	**b**	e	l	t	n	u
c	v	**r**	i	b	b	o	n	s	t	j	a
w	**e**	a	r	r	i	n	g	s	d	q	z

Write.

1 glasses
2 _____
3 _____ 4 _____
5 _____ 6 _____
7 _____
8 _____

2 Look, read and write.

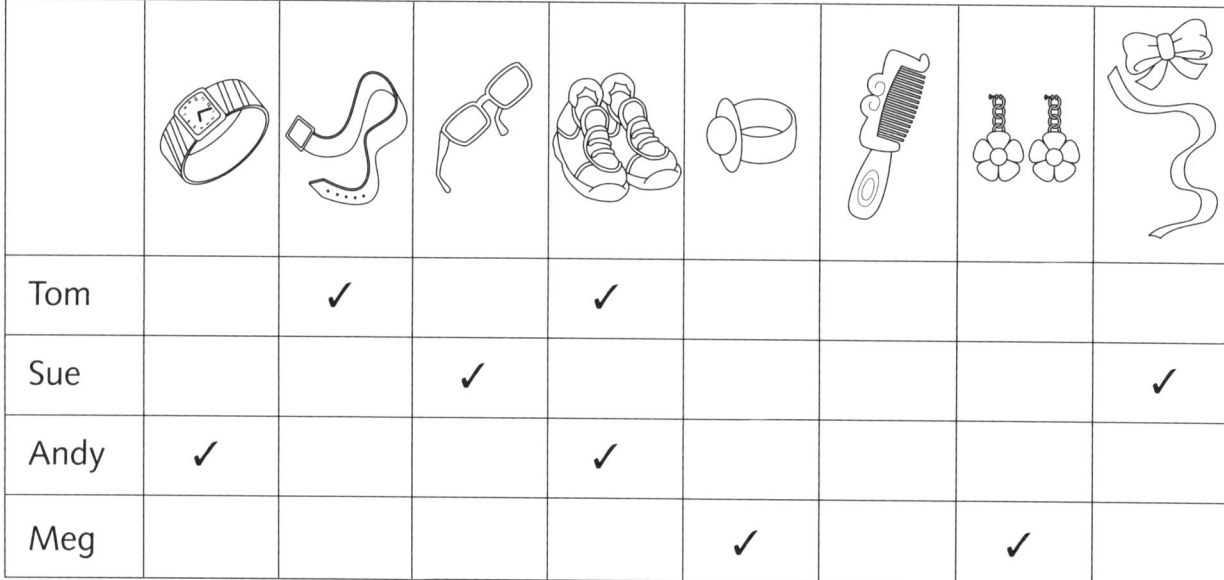

1 Tom has a new belt and new _____.

2 Sue has new _____ and new _____.

3 Andy has a new _____ and new _____.

4 Meg has a new _____ and new _____.

Identifying possessions

3 Write.

yours   mine   hers   his

Meg: Whose ruler is this? Is it _yours_, Sue?

Sue: No, it isn't.

Meg: Is this book _____?

Sue: Yes. It is _____.

Meg: Are these trainers Andy's?

Sue: Yes. They are _____.

Meg: Whose pencil is this? Is it Polly's?

Sue: No, it isn't _____. It's mine.

4 Write.

1 What do they speak in America?
  They speak _____.

2 Where do penguins live?
  They live in _____.

3 Do you have any brothers or sisters?
  _____.

4 When is your birthday?
  It is in _____.

6 Do you have any sweets?
  _____.

5 What is this?
  It is a _____.

7 Does your friend have any sweets?
  _____.

16 What is he doing?

1 Write.   He   She   It   sing   play   walk   sleep   talk

1 What is Mr Macaroni doing? <u>He</u> is <u>singing</u>.
2 What is Tom doing? _____ is _____ basketball.
3 What is Meg doing? _____ is _____ to school.
4 What is the cat doing? _____ is _____.
5 What is Sue doing? _____ is _____ to a friend.

2 Write.   walk   sleep   sing   talk   play

1 Mr Macaroni is <u>sleeping</u>.
2 He is <u>not talking</u> to his friends.
3 He is _____ to work now.
4 He is _____ the piano now.
5 He is _____ now.

3 Write.   Yes, he is.   No, he isn't.   Yes, she is.   No, she isn't.

1 Is Mr Macaroni singing? _____

2 Is he sleeping? _____

3 Is Meg playing basketball? _____

4 Is Meg playing tennis? _____

5 Is Andy playing basketball? _____

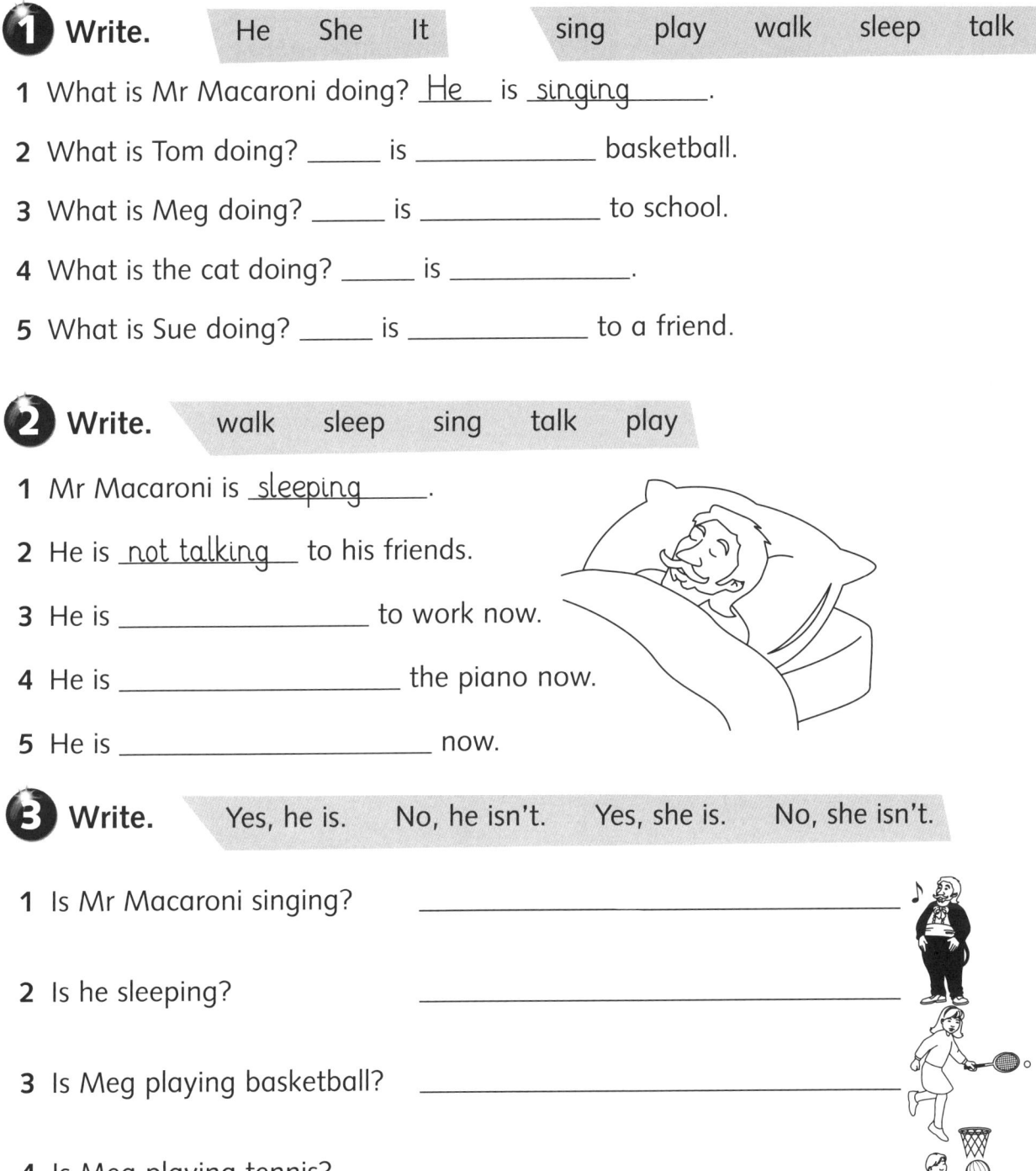

Present continuous: singular

4 Write and colour. am   is   are

1 What are you wearing, Tom?   I _am_ wearing black shoes.

2 What is Andy wearing?
He _____ wearing brown shoes.

3 What are Sue and Meg wearing?
They _____ wearing red shoes.

4 What is Polly wearing?
She _____ wearing blue shoes.

5 Write.   he   she   him   his   her   playing   reading

1 Where is Tom?
Can you see _____?

Yes, I can see _____. _____ has _____ football. _____ likes _____ football.

2 Where is Meg?
Can you see _____?

Yes, I can see _____. _____ has _____ book. _____ likes _____.

6 Write.   riding   eating   sitting   looking   reading   swimming

1 Tom is _swimming_ in the sea.
2 Andy is _____ an apple.
3 Polly is _____ under a tree.
4 Sue is _____ a horse.
5 Meg is _____ at Sue.
6 Pete is _____ a book.

Present continuous: interrogative

Revision Unit 16

1 Read, look and write.   She   He   playing   reading   looking

1 What is Sue doing? _____ basketball.
2 What is Andy doing? _____.
3 What is Polly doing? _____ computer games.
4 What is Pete doing? _____ a book.
5 What is Meg doing? _____ at a fish.

2 Write and colour.

1 <u>Polly is wearing</u> a blue <u>dress</u>.
2 Sue _____ pink trousers and a green _____.
3 _____ grey shorts and a yellow _____.
4 _____ black _____ and a red T-shirt.
5 _____ an orange _____ and a white T-shirt.

3 Write the questions and the answers.   is   isn't

1 Is Andy playing tennis?   No, he _____.
2 Is Polly _____ computer games?   Yes, she _____.
3 _____?   _____
4 _____?   _____
5 _____?   _____

Revision Unit 16

17 We are swimming.

1 Write. looking   eating   riding   swimming   sleeping   singing

1 Meg is at home. She is __looking__ at a book.

2 Mr Macaroni is at work. He is _____.

3 Tom and Andy are at the beach. They are _____.

4 Roz is in the park. She is _____ her bike.

5 Bob and Sam are in the cafe. They are _____ ice cream.

6 The cat is in its basket. It is _____.

2 Read and find.   Write.

w	d	g	s	n	o	w	i	n	g	n
v	s	h	i	n	i	n	g	h	n	t
f	r	a	i	n	i	n	g	h	i	k

1 _____
2 _____
3 _____

3 Write.

1 It is hot. The sun is _____.

2 It is cold. It is _____.

3 It is very cold. It is _____.

Present continuous/describing weather

4 Look and write.

sun – shining   Meg – sitting – umbrella   Tom and Andy – playing football
Pete – swimming – sea   Polly – making – castle   Sue – eating – ice cream

The children are on holiday. The sun (1)_____. Meg (2)_____
under (3)_____. Tom and Andy (4)_____.
Pete (5)_____. Polly (6)_____.
Sue (7)_____.

5 Look and write.

raining   cat – sitting – tree   Meg – looking – cat
Tom – carrying – ladder   bird – singing

Tom and Meg are in the garden. It is (1)_____. The cat (2)_____
in the (3)_____. Meg (4)_____ at the (5)_____.
Tom (6)_____ a (7)_____. The bird (8)_____.

Consolidation

Revision Unit 17

 Look and read. Underline the wrong words.

<u>The sun is shining</u>. The children are <u>walking slowly</u>. They are going to the beach. They are carrying ice creams. They are wearing shoes. They are wearing shorts and T-shirts.

 Write correct sentences.

<u>It is raining. The children are running quickly. They are going to</u>

_____

_____

 Look and write.

sing   1 Look! Mr Macaroni <u>not singing</u>. _____

play football.   2 Tom and Andy <u>are not playing football</u>. _____

sleep   3 _____

riding   4 _____

watching   5 _____

reading   6 _____

It's quarter to eight.

1 Draw.

It's nine o'clock.

It's quarter past eight.

It's half past twelve.

It's quarter to three.

It's eleven o'clock.

It's quarter past one.

2 Read and find.   Write.

q	**a**	r	t	g	**m**	a	t	h	s
s	**s**	p	o	r	t	j	h	g	r
j	l	m	**E**	n	g	l	i	s	h
w	f	**s**	c	i	e	n	c	e	v

1 <u>art</u>   2 _____

3 _____

4 _____

5 _____

3 Write.   reading   counting   looking   drawing   playing

1 They are having sport. They are <u>playing</u> basketball.

2 They are having science. They are _____ at trees.

3 They are having art. They are _____.

4 They are having English. They are _____.

5 They are having maths. They are _____.

Lessons and time **59**

4 Read and find.

q	d	**u**	p	f	**d**	o	w	n	x	t
k	**o**	v	e	r	g	**u**	n	d	e	r
b	f	**t**	h	r	o	u	g	h	y	c
k	**o**	n	t	o	g	**i**	n	t	o	u
k	y	y	**a**	c	r	o	s	s	e	z

Write.

1 _____ 2 _____
3 _____ 4 _____
5 _____
6 _____ 7 _____
8 _____

Write.

through   under   into   over   across   up   down   through

1 The bird is flying <u>through</u> the window.

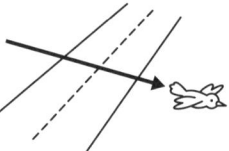

2 It is flying _____ the road.

3 It is flying _____ the trees.

4 It is flying _____ the bridge.

5 It is flying _____ the mountain.

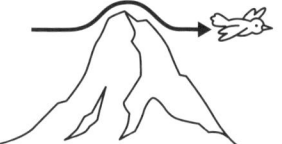

6 It is flying _____ the mountain.

7 It is flying _____ the mountain.

8 It is flying _____ the house.

60   Prepositions

Revision Unit 18

1 Tick (✓) the correct words.

1 across the road ☐
  through the road ☐

2 into the wall ☐
  over the wall ☐

3 through the window ☐
  down the window ☐

4 over the chair ☐
  under the chair ☐

5 in the box ☐
  on the box ☐

6 in the box ☐
  on the box ☐

7 over the hill ☐
  up the hill ☐

8 down the hill ☐
  across the hill ☐

9 through the cafe ☐
  into the café ☐

2 Look and write. What is the time? What are they having?

1 Music   2 Science   3 Maths   4 English   5 Art

1 It's quarter past _____. They are having _____.

2 It's _____. They _____.

3 _____ _____

4 _____ _____

5 _____ _____

19 She is first!

1 Write.

1st	2nd	3rd	4th
first	_____	_____	_____
5th	6th	7th	8th
_____	_____	_____	_____
9th	10th	11th	12th
_____	_____	_____	_____

2 Write.

1st	2nd	3rd	4th
January	_February_	_____	_____
5th	6th	7th	8th
_____	_____	_____	_____
9th	10th	11th	12th
_____	_____	_____	_____

3 Write.

1 July is the _seventh_ month.   2 February is the _____ month.

3 October is the _____ month.   4 March is the _____ month.

5 May is the _____ month.   6 June is the _____ month.

7 December is the _____ month.   8 January is the _____ month.

Ordinal numbers

4 Match and write.

under   down   across   on   up   over   next to   through

1 sitting _on_   **2** jumping _____   **3** standing _____   **4** walking _____

5 running _____   **6** hopping _____   **7** looking _____   **8** swimming _____

5 Look and write.

1 In the _first_ picture _they are sitting on_ the gate.

2 In the _second_ picture _he is jumping over_ the wall.

3 In the _____ picture _____ the tree.

4 In the _____ picture _____ the tree.

5 In the _____ picture _____ the hill.

6 In the _____ picture _____ the hill.

7 In the _____ picture _____ the window.

8 In the _____ picture _____ the river.

Revision Unit 19

1 Read. Write the numbers and the names.

A   B   C   D   E   F

_____ _____ _____ _____ _____ _____

_____ _____ _____ _____ _____ _____

The first girl has short straight hair. Her name is Milly.
The second girl is wearing glasses. Her name is Pam.
The third girl has long straight hair. Her name is Kate.
The fourth girl has short curly hair. Her name is Leila.
The fifth girl is wearing ribbons. Her name is Jo.
The sixth girl is has long curly hair. Her name is Minnie.

2 Look, circle and write the number.

(January)FebruaryMarchAprilMayJuneJulyAugustSeptemberOctoberNovemberDecember
1

3 Read and tick (✓) or cross (✗).

November   January   December   May   October   September

Ron   Ben   Anna   Pat   Jim   Sam

1 Ben's birthday is in the seventh month. ☐
2 Sam's birthday is in the ninth month. ☐
3 Anna's birthday is in the twelfth month. ☐
4 Pat's birthday is in the eighth month. ☐
5 Ron's birthday is in the tenth month. ☐
6 Jim's birthday is in the tenth month. ☐

Revision Unit 19

20 What can you do in English?

1 Name six animals.

_____   _____

_____   _____

_____   _____

2 Write.

1 two _____   four _____   eight _____
   twelve _____   sixteen _____   twenty

2 ten _____   _____   thirty _____
   fifty _____   seventy _____   ninety _____

3 Write the days of the week.

Monday _____   Wednesday _____   Friday

_____   Sunday

4 Name six fruits.

_____   _____

_____   _____

_____   _____

5 Write the alphabet.

A __ C __ E __ G __ I __ K __ M __ O __ Q __ S __ U __ W __ Y __

__ b __ d __ f __ h __ j __ l __ n __ p __ r __ t __ v __ x __ z

Consolidation 65

6 Write. ride sit eat jump play hop

The children (1) _are playing_ in the park. Tom and Andy (2)_____ football. Meg (3)_____ under the tree. Sue (4)_____ an apple. Pete and Billy (5)_____ their bikes. Polly (6)_____ on the slide. Jane (7)_____ over the dinosaur.

How many children are playing in the park? (8)_____

Now you. Write about the picture.

_____

_____

7 Write and answer. Who What How Where Whose When

1 _____ is your name? _____.

2 _____ time do you get up? _____ o'clock.

3 _____ time do you go to bed? _____ o'clock.

4 _____ book is this? It is my book.

5 _____ is your friend? _____ is my friend.

6 _____ do you watch TV? _____ o'clock.

7 _____ do pandas come from? _____.

66 Consolidation

Revision Unit 20

1 Read, write and colour.

wearing playing riding
eating carrying looking

Tom (1)_____ an orange umbrella. Polly (2)_____ a pink ice cream. Pete (3)_____ shorts and a white T-shirt. He (4)_____ at a big book. Andy (5)_____ a brown horse. Meg (6)_____ at a black horse. Sue (7)_____ with a red ball.

2 Write the questions.

1 _____ It is Pete's.

2 _____ It is orange.

3 _____ There is one horse.

4 _____ It is an ice cream.

3 What is wrong? Look and write.

1 Tom is not carrying an umbrella.
He is carrying a box   .

2 Polly _____ an apple.
She _____ an ice cream.

3 _____ a donkey.
_____

4 _____ a kite.
_____

Revision Unit 20 **67**

Handwriting practice

Trace and copy. Revision: capital and small letter formation

Aa   Bb   Cc   Dd

Ee   Ff   Gg   Hh

Ii   Jj   Kk   Ll

Mm   Nn   Oo   Pp

Qq   Rr   Ss   Tt

Uu   Vv   Ww   Xx

Yy   Zz

Trace and copy these patterns.

Trace and copy.

Practice: capital letters and full stops.

I like elephants.

They have big ears.

They have long noses.

They walk slowly.

Trace and copy this poem.

I can see

a very small bee

in the tall green tree

in front of me.

Handwriting practice 71

Trace and copy.

Practice: capital letters, full stops and commas

We like lions and zebras, too.

He likes cats, dogs and frogs.

I want a melon, please.

Look, Meg. It's a whale.

Trace and copy.

Practice: capital letters, full stops, question marks and apostrophes

Is it raining this morning?

No, it isn't. It's sunny.

Is the sun shining today?

No it isn't. It's cold and wet.

Handwriting practice

Trace and copy the questions.

Do you like ice cream?

Does Sam like lollipops?

What is the time, please?

Can you count to a hundred?

Handwriting practice

Copy the story.

The cat on the wall is black.

The mouse under the wall is grey.

Can the cat see the mouse?

No, it can't. Goodbye, mouse!

Trace and copy this information.

Linda lives in London.

It is a very big city.

You can ride on a red bus.

You can see a very big clock.

Trace and copy the story.

On Monday we make a snowman.

On Tuesday he stands still all day.

On Wednesday the sun shines brightly.

On Thursday .... where is our snowman?

Copy this information.

Pandas come from China.

They are black and white.

They have very sharp teeth.

They live in mountains.

They walk across the snow.

Copy the poem.

We like playing in the sun,

running, jumping, having fun.

How many little boats can you see?

John says there are twenty-three.

Copy.

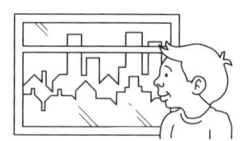

Lots of people work in our town.

There are shopkeepers, waiters

and teachers. Doctors and nurses

work in the hospital. There are lots

of cars and buses, too. Our town is

not quiet, but I like it.